50 Snacks On-the-Go Recipes

By: Kelly Johnson

Table of Contents

- Trail Mix with Nuts and Dried Fruit
- Energy Bites with Oats and Peanut Butter
- Greek Yogurt Parfaits
- Apple Slices with Almond Butter
- Veggie Sticks with Hummus
- Granola Bars
- Banana Bread Muffins
- Rice Cake with Avocado and Egg
- Almond and Coconut Protein Balls
- Roasted Chickpeas
- Smoothie Packs
- Baked Sweet Potato Chips
- Peanut Butter and Banana Wraps
- Overnight Oats Jars
- Mini Quiche Bites
- Chia Pudding Cups
- Homemade Popcorn
- Trail Mix Energy Bars
- Hard-Boiled Eggs
- Veggie Wraps
- Chocolate Dipped Strawberries
- Zucchini Muffins
- Fruit and Nut Energy Bars
- Carrot and Cucumber Sticks with Tzatziki
- Apple Nachos with Almond Butter and Granola
- Dark Chocolate and Nut Clusters
- Frozen Yogurt Bark
- Mini Pita Pockets with Hummus
- Baked Avocado Fries
- Protein-Packed Smoothie
- Cucumber and Cream Cheese Sandwiches
- Oatmeal Energy Bars
- Cacao Energy Balls
- Apple and Cheese Slices
- Cottage Cheese and Pineapple Cups

- Rice Crackers with Tuna Salad
- Dried Fruit and Nut Mix
- Edamame with Sea Salt
- Veggie Frittata Muffins
- Baked Apple Chips
- Sweet Potato Hummus
- Homemade Granola Clusters
- Avocado Toast with Seeds
- Frozen Banana Bites
- Roasted Almonds with Cinnamon
- Coconut Yogurt with Berries
- Protein Smoothie Popsicles
- Cashew and Cranberry Mix
- Mini Veggie Pizzas on English Muffins
- Rice Pudding Cups

Trail Mix with Nuts and Dried Fruit

Ingredients:

- 1 cup almonds
- 1 cup cashews
- 1 cup walnuts
- 1 cup dried cranberries
- 1 cup dried apricots, chopped
- 1/2 cup sunflower seeds
- 1/2 cup pumpkin seeds
- 1/2 cup dark chocolate chips (optional)

Instructions:

1. **Prepare Ingredients:** In a large bowl, combine all nuts, dried fruits, and seeds.
2. **Mix:** Stir together until evenly mixed.
3. **Add Chocolate:** If using, fold in dark chocolate chips.
4. **Store:** Store in an airtight container at room temperature for up to 2 weeks.

Energy Bites with Oats and Peanut Butter

Ingredients:

- 1 cup rolled oats
- 1/2 cup peanut butter
- 1/4 cup honey or maple syrup
- 1/4 cup ground flaxseed
- 1/4 cup mini chocolate chips (optional)
- 1 teaspoon vanilla extract

Instructions:

1. **Mix Ingredients:** In a bowl, combine oats, peanut butter, honey, flaxseed, chocolate chips (if using), and vanilla extract.
2. **Shape into Balls:** Roll the mixture into bite-sized balls (about 1 inch in diameter).
3. **Chill:** Place energy bites on a parchment-lined baking sheet and chill in the refrigerator for at least 30 minutes to set.
4. **Store:** Keep energy bites in an airtight container in the fridge for up to 1 week.

Greek Yogurt Parfaits

Ingredients:

- 2 cups Greek yogurt (plain or flavored)
- 1 cup granola
- 1 cup mixed fresh berries (strawberries, blueberries, raspberries)
- 2 tablespoons honey or maple syrup (optional)

Instructions:

1. **Layer Parfait:** In small jars or glasses, layer Greek yogurt, granola, and mixed berries.
2. **Repeat Layers:** Repeat layers until you run out of ingredients, finishing with a layer of yogurt and fruit on top.
3. **Top with Honey:** Drizzle with honey or maple syrup if desired.
4. **Serve:** Serve immediately, or refrigerate for up to 24 hours.

Apple Slices with Almond Butter

Ingredients:

- 2 apples, cored and sliced
- 1/4 cup almond butter (or peanut butter)
- A sprinkle of cinnamon (optional)

Instructions:

1. **Slice Apples:** Core and slice the apples into wedges.
2. **Serve with Almond Butter:** Arrange apple slices on a plate and serve with almond butter on the side for dipping.
3. **Optional Cinnamon:** Sprinkle cinnamon on top of the apple slices for added flavor.

Veggie Sticks with Hummus

Ingredients:

- 1 cucumber, cut into sticks
- 1 carrot, peeled and cut into sticks
- 1 bell pepper, sliced into strips
- 1/2 cup hummus

Instructions:

1. **Prepare Veggies:** Cut the cucumber, carrot, and bell pepper into sticks or strips.
2. **Serve with Hummus:** Arrange the veggies on a plate and serve with hummus for dipping.

Granola Bars

Ingredients:

- 2 cups rolled oats
- 1/2 cup honey or maple syrup
- 1/4 cup peanut butter or almond butter
- 1/2 cup dried fruit (raisins, cranberries, apricots)
- 1/4 cup nuts (almonds, walnuts, or cashews)
- 1/4 teaspoon vanilla extract
- A pinch of salt

Instructions:

1. **Mix Wet Ingredients:** In a small saucepan over medium heat, warm the honey (or maple syrup) and peanut butter until melted and well combined. Stir in vanilla extract.
2. **Combine Dry Ingredients:** In a large bowl, combine oats, dried fruit, nuts, and a pinch of salt.
3. **Combine Wet and Dry Ingredients:** Pour the wet mixture over the dry ingredients and stir until evenly combined.
4. **Press into Pan:** Line a baking pan with parchment paper and press the mixture into the pan. Use a spatula to compress it tightly.
5. **Chill and Slice:** Chill the mixture in the fridge for at least 2 hours, then slice into bars.
6. **Store:** Store in an airtight container for up to a week.

Banana Bread Muffins

Ingredients:

- 2 ripe bananas, mashed
- 1/2 cup vegetable oil or melted butter
- 1/2 cup brown sugar
- 1 egg
- 1 teaspoon vanilla extract
- 1 1/2 cups all-purpose flour
- 1 teaspoon baking soda
- 1/2 teaspoon salt
- 1/2 teaspoon cinnamon (optional)

Instructions:

1. **Preheat Oven:** Preheat the oven to 350°F (175°C) and line a muffin tin with paper liners.
2. **Mix Wet Ingredients:** In a bowl, combine mashed bananas, oil, brown sugar, egg, and vanilla extract.
3. **Combine Dry Ingredients:** In another bowl, mix flour, baking soda, salt, and cinnamon.
4. **Combine Wet and Dry Ingredients:** Stir the dry ingredients into the wet ingredients until just combined.
5. **Fill Muffin Tin:** Spoon the batter into the muffin tin, filling each cup about 2/3 full.
6. **Bake:** Bake for 18-20 minutes, or until a toothpick comes out clean. Let cool before serving.

Rice Cake with Avocado and Egg

Ingredients:

- 1 rice cake (plain or whole grain)
- 1/2 avocado, sliced
- 1 hard-boiled egg, sliced
- Salt and pepper to taste
- A sprinkle of red pepper flakes (optional)

Instructions:

1. **Prepare the Rice Cake:** Place the rice cake on a plate.
2. **Top with Avocado and Egg:** Layer the rice cake with slices of avocado and hard-boiled egg.
3. **Season:** Sprinkle with salt, pepper, and red pepper flakes (if using).
4. **Serve:** Enjoy immediately as a quick and healthy snack.

Almond and Coconut Protein Balls

Ingredients:

- 1 cup almonds
- 1/2 cup shredded coconut (unsweetened)
- 1/4 cup honey or maple syrup
- 2 tablespoons peanut butter or almond butter
- 1/4 cup protein powder (vanilla or chocolate)
- 1 tablespoon chia seeds
- 1 teaspoon vanilla extract

Instructions:

1. **Blend Almonds:** In a food processor, blend the almonds until finely chopped.
2. **Combine Ingredients:** Add shredded coconut, honey, peanut butter, protein powder, chia seeds, and vanilla extract. Process until the mixture sticks together.
3. **Roll into Balls:** Roll the mixture into bite-sized balls (about 1 inch).
4. **Chill:** Place the protein balls on a parchment-lined tray and chill in the fridge for 30 minutes to set.
5. **Store:** Store in an airtight container in the fridge for up to a week.

Roasted Chickpeas

Ingredients:

- 1 can (15 oz) chickpeas, drained and rinsed
- 1 tablespoon olive oil
- 1 teaspoon smoked paprika
- 1/2 teaspoon garlic powder
- Salt and pepper, to taste

Instructions:

1. **Preheat Oven:** Preheat the oven to 400°F (200°C).
2. **Prepare Chickpeas:** Pat the chickpeas dry with paper towels to remove excess moisture.
3. **Season:** Toss the chickpeas with olive oil, smoked paprika, garlic powder, salt, and pepper.
4. **Roast:** Spread the chickpeas in a single layer on a baking sheet and roast for 25-30 minutes, stirring halfway through, until crispy.
5. **Cool and Serve:** Let cool before serving. Store in an airtight container for up to a week.

Smoothie Packs

Ingredients (for one pack):

- 1/2 cup frozen spinach or kale
- 1/2 cup frozen mixed berries
- 1/2 banana
- 1 tablespoon chia seeds or flaxseeds
- 1/4 cup Greek yogurt or protein powder
- 1/2 cup almond milk or milk of choice

Instructions:

1. **Assemble Smoothie Packs:** In a freezer-safe bag or container, layer the ingredients: spinach, berries, banana, seeds, and yogurt (or protein powder).
2. **Freeze:** Seal the bag/container and freeze for up to a month.
3. **Blend:** When ready to use, blend the smoothie pack with almond milk (or your preferred liquid) until smooth.
4. **Serve:** Enjoy a healthy smoothie anytime!

Baked Sweet Potato Chips

Ingredients:

- 2 medium sweet potatoes, thinly sliced
- 1 tablespoon olive oil
- 1/2 teaspoon salt
- 1/2 teaspoon smoked paprika or cinnamon (optional)

Instructions:

1. **Preheat Oven:** Preheat the oven to 400°F (200°C).
2. **Prepare Sweet Potatoes:** Slice the sweet potatoes into thin rounds using a mandolin or sharp knife.
3. **Season:** Toss the sweet potato slices with olive oil, salt, and any additional seasonings.
4. **Bake:** Spread the slices in a single layer on a baking sheet. Bake for 20-25 minutes, flipping halfway through, until crispy.
5. **Cool and Serve:** Let the chips cool on a wire rack before serving.

Peanut Butter and Banana Wraps

Ingredients:

- 1 whole wheat or flour tortilla
- 2 tablespoons peanut butter
- 1 banana, sliced
- A drizzle of honey (optional)

Instructions:

1. **Spread Peanut Butter:** Lay the tortilla flat and spread the peanut butter evenly across it.
2. **Add Banana Slices:** Arrange banana slices over the peanut butter.
3. **Wrap and Serve:** Roll up the tortilla and slice into smaller pieces if desired. Drizzle with honey if you like extra sweetness.

Overnight Oats Jars

Ingredients (for one jar):

- 1/2 cup rolled oats
- 1/2 cup almond milk or milk of choice
- 1 tablespoon chia seeds
- 1/2 teaspoon vanilla extract
- 1/2 teaspoon maple syrup (optional)
- Toppings: fresh fruit, nuts, or seeds

Instructions:

1. **Assemble Jars:** In a mason jar or airtight container, combine oats, almond milk, chia seeds, vanilla extract, and maple syrup.
2. **Refrigerate:** Seal the jar/container and refrigerate overnight (or for at least 4 hours).
3. **Top and Serve:** In the morning, top with fresh fruit, nuts, or seeds and enjoy.

Mini Quiche Bites

Ingredients:

- 1/2 cup milk
- 3 large eggs
- 1/2 cup shredded cheese (cheddar, mozzarella, or your choice)
- 1/4 cup cooked spinach, drained (or other vegetables like mushrooms or bell peppers)
- Salt and pepper, to taste

Instructions:

1. **Preheat Oven:** Preheat the oven to 350°F (175°C).
2. **Prepare Filling:** In a bowl, whisk together the eggs and milk. Stir in the cheese, spinach, and seasonings.
3. **Fill Muffin Tin:** Grease a mini muffin tin and pour the egg mixture into each cup, filling them about 3/4 full.
4. **Bake:** Bake for 12-15 minutes, or until the quiche bites are set and lightly golden.
5. **Cool and Serve:** Let cool slightly before serving. Store leftovers in the fridge for up to 3 days.

Chia Pudding Cups

Ingredients (for one cup):

- 3 tablespoons chia seeds
- 1/2 cup almond milk (or milk of choice)
- 1/2 teaspoon vanilla extract
- 1 teaspoon maple syrup or honey (optional)
- Toppings: fresh berries, nuts, coconut flakes

Instructions:

1. **Combine Ingredients:** In a small bowl or jar, mix chia seeds, almond milk, vanilla extract, and sweetener.
2. **Refrigerate:** Stir well, then cover and refrigerate overnight or for at least 4 hours to thicken.
3. **Top and Serve:** Before serving, top with fresh berries, nuts, or coconut flakes.

Homemade Popcorn

Ingredients:

- 1/4 cup popcorn kernels
- 1 tablespoon olive oil or butter
- Salt, to taste
- Optional: melted butter, cheese, or seasoning of your choice (e.g., garlic powder, nutritional yeast)

Instructions:

1. **Heat Oil:** Heat the olive oil or butter in a large pot over medium heat.
2. **Pop the Kernels:** Add the popcorn kernels to the pot and cover. Shake the pot occasionally to ensure the kernels don't burn. Once the popping slows down, remove from heat.
3. **Season:** Pour the popcorn into a bowl and sprinkle with salt or any seasoning you prefer. For extra flavor, drizzle with melted butter or sprinkle cheese.
4. **Serve:** Enjoy the popcorn immediately!

Trail Mix Energy Bars

Ingredients:

- 1 cup rolled oats
- 1/2 cup mixed nuts (almonds, walnuts, cashews), chopped
- 1/4 cup dried fruit (raisins, cranberries, apricots), chopped
- 1/4 cup honey or maple syrup
- 2 tablespoons peanut butter or almond butter
- 1 teaspoon vanilla extract
- Pinch of salt
- Optional: 1/4 cup dark chocolate chips

Instructions:

1. **Mix Dry Ingredients:** In a large bowl, combine oats, chopped nuts, dried fruit, and a pinch of salt.
2. **Combine Wet Ingredients:** In a small saucepan, heat honey (or maple syrup) and peanut butter over low heat until melted and smooth. Stir in vanilla extract.
3. **Combine:** Pour the wet mixture over the dry ingredients and mix until everything is well coated.
4. **Press and Chill:** Press the mixture into a lined baking pan (8x8-inch) and refrigerate for at least 2 hours to set.
5. **Cut and Serve:** Once set, cut into bars and enjoy!

Hard-Boiled Eggs

Ingredients:

- 6 large eggs

Instructions:

1. **Boil Water:** Place eggs in a saucepan and cover with cold water. Bring the water to a boil over medium-high heat.
2. **Cook the Eggs:** Once boiling, reduce heat to low and simmer for 9-12 minutes (9 minutes for slightly soft yolks, 12 minutes for firm yolks).
3. **Cool:** Remove the eggs from the saucepan and place them in a bowl of ice water for 5 minutes to cool.
4. **Peel and Serve:** Peel the eggs and season with salt and pepper. Enjoy as a snack or slice for salads.

Veggie Wraps

Ingredients:

- 1 large tortilla or wrap
- 1/2 cup hummus or cream cheese
- 1/2 cup mixed greens (spinach, lettuce, arugula)
- 1/4 cup shredded carrots
- 1/4 cucumber, sliced
- 1/4 avocado, sliced
- Salt and pepper, to taste

Instructions:

1. **Spread Base:** Spread a layer of hummus or cream cheese on the tortilla.
2. **Assemble Veggies:** Layer on the mixed greens, shredded carrots, cucumber, and avocado slices.
3. **Wrap:** Sprinkle with salt and pepper, then fold in the sides of the tortilla and roll it up tightly.
4. **Serve:** Slice the wrap into halves and serve immediately.

Chocolate Dipped Strawberries

Ingredients:

- 12 fresh strawberries, washed and dried
- 1/2 cup dark chocolate or milk chocolate chips
- Optional: sprinkles, crushed nuts, or coconut flakes for topping

Instructions:

1. **Melt Chocolate:** Melt the chocolate chips in a microwave-safe bowl, stirring every 30 seconds until smooth.
2. **Dip Strawberries:** Hold each strawberry by the stem and dip it into the melted chocolate, covering about 3/4 of the berry.
3. **Optional Toppings:** Roll the dipped strawberries in sprinkles, crushed nuts, or coconut flakes, if desired.
4. **Chill:** Place the dipped strawberries on a parchment-lined tray and refrigerate for 15-20 minutes until the chocolate hardens.
5. **Serve:** Enjoy as a delicious treat!

Zucchini Muffins

Ingredients:

- 1 1/2 cups grated zucchini (about 1 medium zucchini)
- 1 1/2 cups flour (all-purpose or whole wheat)
- 1/2 teaspoon baking soda
- 1/2 teaspoon baking powder
- 1 teaspoon cinnamon
- 1/2 teaspoon vanilla extract
- 1/2 cup sugar or maple syrup
- 1/4 cup olive oil or vegetable oil
- 2 eggs

Instructions:

1. **Preheat Oven:** Preheat the oven to 350°F (175°C) and grease a muffin tin or line with paper liners.
2. **Mix Dry Ingredients:** In a bowl, combine the flour, baking soda, baking powder, and cinnamon.
3. **Mix Wet Ingredients:** In another bowl, whisk the eggs, sugar, vanilla extract, and olive oil.
4. **Combine and Fold:** Add the grated zucchini to the wet ingredients, then fold in the dry ingredients until just combined.
5. **Fill Muffin Tin:** Divide the batter among the muffin cups, filling each about 2/3 full.
6. **Bake:** Bake for 20-25 minutes or until a toothpick inserted into the center comes out clean.
7. **Cool and Serve:** Let cool before serving.

Fruit and Nut Energy Bars

Ingredients:

- 1 cup mixed nuts (almonds, cashews, walnuts), chopped
- 1/2 cup dried fruit (raisins, cranberries, apricots), chopped
- 1/4 cup oats
- 2 tablespoons honey or maple syrup
- 2 tablespoons peanut butter or almond butter
- 1 teaspoon vanilla extract
- Pinch of salt

Instructions:

1. **Mix Dry Ingredients:** In a bowl, combine the chopped nuts, dried fruit, and oats.
2. **Combine Wet Ingredients:** In a small saucepan, heat the honey and peanut butter until melted and smooth. Stir in the vanilla extract and pinch of salt.
3. **Combine:** Pour the wet ingredients over the dry mixture and stir until everything is well combined.
4. **Press and Chill:** Press the mixture into a lined baking dish or pan and refrigerate for at least 2 hours.
5. **Cut and Serve:** Once chilled, cut into bars and enjoy!

Carrot and Cucumber Sticks with Tzatziki

Ingredients:

- 2 medium carrots, peeled and sliced into sticks
- 1 cucumber, sliced into sticks
- 1/2 cup tzatziki sauce (store-bought or homemade)

Instructions:

1. **Prepare Veggies:** Peel and slice the carrots and cucumber into sticks.
2. **Serve:** Arrange the veggie sticks on a platter or in individual serving cups.
3. **Dip:** Serve with tzatziki sauce for dipping.

Apple Nachos with Almond Butter and Granola

Ingredients:

- 2 apples, sliced thinly
- 2 tablespoons almond butter (or peanut butter)
- 1/4 cup granola
- 2 tablespoons raisins or dried cranberries (optional)
- Drizzle of honey (optional)
- A pinch of cinnamon (optional)

Instructions:

1. **Prepare Apples:** Slice the apples into thin rounds and arrange them on a plate or tray.
2. **Drizzle Almond Butter:** Warm the almond butter in the microwave for 15-20 seconds, then drizzle it over the apple slices.
3. **Top with Granola:** Sprinkle granola over the apples and top with raisins or dried cranberries if using.
4. **Finish:** Drizzle with honey and sprinkle cinnamon on top, if desired.
5. **Serve:** Enjoy immediately as a sweet and healthy snack!

Dark Chocolate and Nut Clusters

Ingredients:

- 1/2 cup mixed nuts (almonds, cashews, walnuts), roughly chopped
- 1/2 cup dark chocolate chips or chopped dark chocolate
- 1/4 cup dried fruit (raisins, cranberries, or apricots), optional
- A pinch of sea salt (optional)

Instructions:

1. **Melt Chocolate:** In a microwave-safe bowl, melt the dark chocolate in 20-30 second intervals, stirring in between until smooth.
2. **Mix Nuts and Fruit:** Stir the chopped nuts (and dried fruit, if using) into the melted chocolate until well coated.
3. **Form Clusters:** Drop spoonfuls of the mixture onto a parchment-lined tray, forming clusters.
4. **Chill:** Refrigerate the clusters for 15-30 minutes or until the chocolate hardens.
5. **Serve:** Enjoy the clusters as a sweet and crunchy snack.

Frozen Yogurt Bark

Ingredients:

- 2 cups Greek yogurt
- 1-2 tablespoons honey or maple syrup
- 1/4 cup granola
- 1/4 cup fresh berries (blueberries, raspberries, strawberries)
- 2 tablespoons dark chocolate chips or dried fruit (optional)

Instructions:

1. **Mix Yogurt:** In a bowl, combine the Greek yogurt and honey (or maple syrup) and stir until smooth.
2. **Spread Yogurt:** Spread the yogurt mixture evenly on a baking sheet lined with parchment paper.
3. **Add Toppings:** Sprinkle granola, berries, and any other toppings (chocolate chips, dried fruit) over the yogurt.
4. **Freeze:** Freeze the yogurt bark for at least 2 hours, or until completely frozen.
5. **Break into Pieces:** Once frozen, break the bark into pieces and serve immediately.

Mini Pita Pockets with Hummus

Ingredients:

- 4 small whole wheat pita pockets
- 1/2 cup hummus (store-bought or homemade)
- 1/4 cup sliced cucumber
- 1/4 cup sliced cherry tomatoes
- A handful of mixed greens (spinach, arugula, or lettuce)
- A pinch of salt and pepper

Instructions:

1. **Prepare Pita:** Slice each pita pocket in half to create 2 mini pockets.
2. **Fill Pita:** Spread a generous tablespoon of hummus inside each pita half.
3. **Add Veggies:** Fill each pocket with cucumber, tomatoes, and mixed greens.
4. **Season:** Sprinkle with salt and pepper to taste.
5. **Serve:** Enjoy these light and healthy pita pockets as a snack or light lunch.

Baked Avocado Fries

Ingredients:

- 2 ripe avocados, sliced into wedges
- 1/2 cup breadcrumbs (preferably whole wheat)
- 1/4 cup grated Parmesan cheese (optional)
- 1 teaspoon garlic powder
- 1/2 teaspoon paprika
- 1 egg, beaten
- Salt and pepper, to taste

Instructions:

1. **Preheat Oven:** Preheat your oven to 400°F (200°C) and line a baking sheet with parchment paper.
2. **Prepare Breading:** In one shallow bowl, mix the breadcrumbs, Parmesan cheese, garlic powder, paprika, salt, and pepper.
3. **Dip Avocado:** Dip each avocado wedge into the beaten egg, then coat in the breadcrumb mixture.
4. **Bake:** Arrange the coated avocado wedges on the baking sheet and bake for 15-20 minutes, or until golden and crispy.
5. **Serve:** Enjoy the crispy avocado fries with a dipping sauce, such as ranch or salsa.

Protein-Packed Smoothie

Ingredients:

- 1 banana
- 1/2 cup Greek yogurt
- 1 tablespoon peanut butter or almond butter
- 1/2 cup milk (dairy or plant-based)
- 1 tablespoon chia seeds or flax seeds
- 1/2 cup spinach (optional)
- Ice cubes (optional)

Instructions:

1. **Blend Ingredients:** Combine all the ingredients in a blender.
2. **Blend Smooth:** Blend until smooth, adding more milk if needed to reach the desired consistency.
3. **Serve:** Pour into a glass and enjoy your protein-packed smoothie!

Cucumber and Cream Cheese Sandwiches

Ingredients:

- 1 cucumber, thinly sliced
- 8 slices whole grain or white bread
- 4 tablespoons cream cheese (plain or herbed)
- Fresh dill or parsley, for garnish (optional)
- Salt and pepper, to taste

Instructions:

1. **Spread Cream Cheese:** Spread a thin layer of cream cheese on each slice of bread.
2. **Layer Cucumber:** Arrange the cucumber slices on top of the cream cheese.
3. **Season:** Sprinkle with salt, pepper, and fresh dill or parsley for extra flavor.
4. **Assemble Sandwiches:** Top with another slice of bread to form a sandwich.
5. **Serve:** Cut into halves or quarters and serve immediately.

Oatmeal Energy Bars

Ingredients:

- 2 cups rolled oats
- 1/2 cup nut butter (peanut butter or almond butter)
- 1/4 cup honey or maple syrup
- 1/4 cup dried fruit (raisins, cranberries, or apricots), chopped
- 1/4 cup mini chocolate chips (optional)
- 1 tablespoon chia seeds or flax seeds
- 1 teaspoon vanilla extract
- A pinch of salt

Instructions:

1. **Mix Ingredients:** In a large bowl, combine oats, nut butter, honey (or maple syrup), dried fruit, chocolate chips, chia seeds, vanilla extract, and salt. Mix until well combined.
2. **Press into Pan:** Line an 8x8-inch baking pan with parchment paper and press the mixture into the pan evenly.
3. **Chill:** Refrigerate for at least 2 hours or until set.
4. **Cut and Serve:** Once chilled, cut the mixture into bars and enjoy!

Cacao Energy Balls

Ingredients:

- 1 cup rolled oats
- 1/2 cup nut butter (peanut butter, almond butter, or cashew butter)
- 2 tablespoons raw cacao powder
- 2 tablespoons honey or maple syrup
- 1/4 cup dark chocolate chips (optional)
- 1 tablespoon chia seeds or flax seeds (optional)
- Pinch of salt

Instructions:

1. **Combine Ingredients**: In a mixing bowl, combine the oats, nut butter, cacao powder, honey (or maple syrup), chocolate chips, chia seeds (if using), and salt. Stir until everything is well combined.
2. **Form Balls**: Use your hands to roll the mixture into small balls, about 1 inch in diameter.
3. **Chill**: Place the balls on a baking sheet lined with parchment paper and refrigerate for at least 30 minutes to firm up.
4. **Serve**: Once chilled, enjoy your cacao energy balls as a delicious and energizing snack!

Apple and Cheese Slices

Ingredients:

- 1 apple, cored and sliced
- 2 oz cheese (cheddar, gouda, or brie work well)

Instructions:

1. **Prepare Apple**: Slice the apple into thin wedges.
2. **Slice Cheese**: Slice the cheese into small wedges or cubes.
3. **Serve**: Arrange the apple slices and cheese on a plate and enjoy the sweet and savory combination!

Cottage Cheese and Pineapple Cups

Ingredients:

- 1 cup cottage cheese
- 1/2 cup pineapple chunks (fresh or canned, drained)

Instructions:

1. **Assemble**: Spoon the cottage cheese into a bowl or individual serving cups.
2. **Top with Pineapple**: Add the pineapple chunks on top of the cottage cheese.
3. **Serve**: Enjoy immediately, or chill in the fridge for a refreshing snack!

Rice Crackers with Tuna Salad

Ingredients:

- 1 can (5 oz) tuna in water, drained
- 2 tablespoons mayonnaise or Greek yogurt
- 1 tablespoon Dijon mustard (optional)
- Salt and pepper, to taste
- Rice crackers (store-bought or homemade)

Instructions:

1. **Prepare Tuna Salad**: In a bowl, mix the tuna, mayonnaise (or Greek yogurt), Dijon mustard, and a pinch of salt and pepper. Stir until well combined.
2. **Serve**: Spoon the tuna salad onto rice crackers. You can top them with fresh herbs or a squeeze of lemon if desired.
3. **Enjoy**: Serve immediately for a tasty and light snack!

Dried Fruit and Nut Mix

Ingredients:

- 1/2 cup almonds
- 1/2 cup walnuts
- 1/2 cup cashews
- 1/2 cup dried cranberries
- 1/2 cup dried apricots, chopped
- 1/2 cup raisins or golden raisins
- 1/4 cup sunflower seeds (optional)
- A pinch of sea salt (optional)

Instructions:

1. **Mix Ingredients**: In a large bowl, combine the almonds, walnuts, cashews, dried cranberries, apricots, raisins, and sunflower seeds.
2. **Toss and Serve**: Stir everything together until well mixed. Optionally, sprinkle with a pinch of sea salt for a savory twist.
3. **Serve**: Store in an airtight container at room temperature for up to a week. Enjoy as a snack on the go!

Edamame with Sea Salt

Ingredients:

- 1 cup frozen edamame (in pods or shelled)
- 1 tablespoon olive oil (optional)
- Sea salt, to taste

Instructions:

1. **Cook Edamame**: Boil the edamame in salted water for 3-5 minutes (if frozen in pods) or according to package instructions. Alternatively, steam them.
2. **Season**: Drain and toss with a little olive oil if desired, then sprinkle with sea salt.
3. **Serve**: Serve warm as a quick and healthy snack, or chill for later.

Veggie Frittata Muffins

Ingredients:

- 6 large eggs
- 1/2 cup milk (dairy or plant-based)
- 1/2 cup diced bell peppers
- 1/2 cup spinach, chopped
- 1/4 cup diced onions
- 1/4 cup shredded cheese (optional)
- Salt and pepper, to taste
- Olive oil spray for greasing

Instructions:

1. **Preheat Oven**: Preheat your oven to 350°F (175°C). Spray a muffin tin with olive oil.
2. **Prepare Veggies**: Sauté the bell peppers, onions, and spinach in a pan until softened (about 5 minutes).
3. **Mix Eggs**: In a bowl, whisk the eggs, milk, and season with salt and pepper.
4. **Assemble Muffins**: Divide the cooked veggies evenly among the muffin cups. Pour the egg mixture over the veggies, filling each muffin cup.
5. **Bake**: Bake in the preheated oven for 15-20 minutes or until set and slightly golden on top.
6. **Serve**: Allow to cool slightly before serving. These can be stored in the fridge for up to 4 days and enjoyed as a quick snack or breakfast!

Baked Apple Chips

Ingredients:

- 2 large apples (any variety)
- 1 teaspoon cinnamon
- 1 tablespoon lemon juice (optional)

Instructions:

1. **Preheat Oven**: Preheat your oven to 200°F (90°C).
2. **Prepare Apples**: Thinly slice the apples using a mandolin or sharp knife, removing the cores.
3. **Season**: Place apple slices on a baking sheet lined with parchment paper. Sprinkle with cinnamon and lightly drizzle with lemon juice.
4. **Bake**: Bake for 1-2 hours, flipping the slices halfway through, until they are crispy and golden.
5. **Serve**: Let cool before serving. Store in an airtight container for up to a week.

Sweet Potato Hummus

Ingredients:

- 1 medium sweet potato, peeled and diced
- 1 can (15 oz) chickpeas, drained and rinsed
- 2 tablespoons tahini
- 1 tablespoon olive oil
- 1 tablespoon lemon juice
- 1 teaspoon ground cumin
- Salt and pepper, to taste
- A pinch of paprika or chili flakes for garnish (optional)

Instructions:

1. **Cook Sweet Potato**: Boil or roast the diced sweet potato until tender (about 10-15 minutes). If roasting, drizzle with olive oil and bake at 400°F (200°C) for 20 minutes until soft.
2. **Blend Hummus**: In a food processor, combine the cooked sweet potato, chickpeas, tahini, olive oil, lemon juice, cumin, salt, and pepper. Blend until smooth.
3. **Serve**: Garnish with paprika or chili flakes, if desired. Serve with pita, veggie sticks, or crackers.

Homemade Granola Clusters

Ingredients:

- 2 cups rolled oats
- 1/4 cup honey or maple syrup
- 1/4 cup nut butter (peanut butter, almond butter, etc.)
- 1/2 cup mixed nuts (almonds, walnuts, cashews, etc.), chopped
- 1/4 cup dried fruit (raisins, cranberries, etc.)
- 1/4 teaspoon cinnamon
- A pinch of salt

Instructions:

1. **Preheat Oven**: Preheat the oven to 325°F (160°C) and line a baking sheet with parchment paper.
2. **Mix Ingredients**: In a large bowl, combine the oats, honey (or maple syrup), nut butter, nuts, dried fruit, cinnamon, and salt. Stir until well coated.
3. **Bake**: Spread the mixture in a single layer on the baking sheet. Bake for 15-20 minutes, stirring halfway through, until golden and crispy.
4. **Cool and Serve**: Let the granola cool completely before breaking it into clusters. Store in an airtight container.

Avocado Toast with Seeds

Ingredients:

- 1 ripe avocado
- 2 slices whole-grain bread
- 1 tablespoon sunflower seeds, chia seeds, or pumpkin seeds
- Salt and pepper, to taste
- Red pepper flakes or lemon juice (optional)

Instructions:

1. **Toast Bread**: Toast the bread slices until golden and crispy.
2. **Prepare Avocado**: Mash the avocado in a bowl and season with salt, pepper, and optional red pepper flakes or a squeeze of lemon juice.
3. **Assemble Toast**: Spread the mashed avocado evenly onto the toasted bread slices.
4. **Garnish**: Sprinkle with seeds for added crunch and nutrition.
5. **Serve**: Enjoy immediately for a quick and nutritious snack!

Frozen Banana Bites

Ingredients:

- 2 ripe bananas
- 1/4 cup almond butter or peanut butter
- 1/4 cup dark chocolate chips (optional)
- 1 tablespoon coconut flakes (optional)
- A pinch of sea salt (optional)

Instructions:

1. **Slice Bananas**: Slice the bananas into 1/2-inch thick rounds.
2. **Spread Nut Butter**: Spread a small amount of almond or peanut butter onto half of the banana slices.
3. **Sandwich the Bites**: Place the remaining banana slices on top of the nut butter, forming little "sandwiches."
4. **Freeze**: Lay the banana bites on a parchment-lined baking sheet and freeze for about 1 hour, or until firm.
5. **Optional Toppings**: For added flavor, drizzle melted dark chocolate over the bites and sprinkle with coconut flakes or a pinch of sea salt.
6. **Serve**: Serve immediately or store in an airtight container in the freezer for up to a week.

Roasted Almonds with Cinnamon

Ingredients:

- 1 cup raw almonds
- 1 tablespoon olive oil or coconut oil
- 1 teaspoon cinnamon
- 1 tablespoon honey or maple syrup
- A pinch of salt

Instructions:

1. **Preheat Oven**: Preheat the oven to 350°F (175°C) and line a baking sheet with parchment paper.
2. **Toss Almonds**: In a bowl, toss the almonds with olive oil, cinnamon, honey, and salt until they are well coated.
3. **Roast**: Spread the almonds in a single layer on the baking sheet and roast for 10-15 minutes, stirring halfway through, until golden and fragrant.
4. **Cool and Serve**: Allow the almonds to cool completely before serving. Store in an airtight container.

Coconut Yogurt with Berries

Ingredients:

- 1 cup coconut yogurt (or any preferred non-dairy yogurt)
- 1/4 cup fresh mixed berries (blueberries, raspberries, strawberries)
- 1 tablespoon shredded coconut (optional)
- 1 teaspoon honey or maple syrup (optional)

Instructions:

1. **Serve Yogurt**: Spoon the coconut yogurt into a small bowl.
2. **Top with Berries**: Add fresh berries on top of the yogurt.
3. **Optional Toppings**: Sprinkle with shredded coconut and drizzle with honey or maple syrup if desired.
4. **Serve**: Enjoy immediately for a refreshing and healthy snack!

Protein Smoothie Popsicles

Ingredients:

- 1 cup Greek yogurt or plant-based yogurt
- 1/2 cup almond milk (or any milk of choice)
- 1 banana
- 1 scoop protein powder (vanilla or chocolate)
- 1/2 cup mixed berries (optional)
- 1 tablespoon chia seeds or flax seeds (optional)

Instructions:

1. **Blend Ingredients**: In a blender, combine the Greek yogurt, almond milk, banana, protein powder, mixed berries (if using), and chia seeds or flax seeds. Blend until smooth.
2. **Pour into Molds**: Pour the smoothie mixture into popsicle molds.
3. **Freeze**: Freeze for 4-6 hours or until fully set.
4. **Serve**: Run warm water over the outside of the molds to release the popsicles. Enjoy!

Cashew and Cranberry Mix

Ingredients:

- 1 cup raw cashews
- 1/2 cup dried cranberries
- 1 tablespoon sunflower seeds (optional)
- A pinch of sea salt (optional)

Instructions:

1. **Combine Ingredients**: In a bowl, combine the cashews, dried cranberries, and sunflower seeds (if using).
2. **Season**: Sprinkle with a pinch of sea salt for extra flavor (optional).
3. **Serve**: Serve immediately as a healthy snack or store in an airtight container for up to a week.

Mini Veggie Pizzas on English Muffins

Ingredients:

- 4 whole-wheat English muffins, split in half
- 1/2 cup tomato sauce or pizza sauce
- 1 cup shredded mozzarella cheese (or dairy-free cheese)
- 1/2 cup bell peppers, diced
- 1/4 cup red onion, sliced
- 1/4 cup spinach, chopped
- 1/2 teaspoon dried oregano
- Salt and pepper to taste

Instructions:

1. **Preheat Oven**: Preheat your oven to 375°F (190°C).
2. **Prepare English Muffins**: Place the split English muffins on a baking sheet, cut side up.
3. **Top with Sauce**: Spread a thin layer of tomato sauce on each muffin half.
4. **Add Toppings**: Sprinkle with shredded mozzarella cheese and top with diced bell peppers, red onions, spinach, and a sprinkle of oregano, salt, and pepper.
5. **Bake**: Bake for 10-12 minutes, or until the cheese is melted and bubbly.
6. **Serve**: Serve warm and enjoy as a delicious snack or mini meal!

Rice Pudding Cups

Ingredients:

- 1 cup cooked rice (preferably short-grain or Arborio rice)
- 1 1/2 cups milk (dairy or plant-based)
- 2 tablespoons maple syrup or honey
- 1/4 teaspoon vanilla extract
- 1/4 teaspoon ground cinnamon
- A pinch of salt
- Fresh fruit or berries for topping (optional)

Instructions:

1. **Cook Rice**: If not already cooked, prepare rice according to package instructions.
2. **Combine Ingredients**: In a saucepan, combine the cooked rice, milk, maple syrup or honey, vanilla extract, cinnamon, and salt.
3. **Simmer**: Bring the mixture to a gentle simmer over medium heat, stirring occasionally. Cook for about 10-15 minutes, until the rice absorbs some of the liquid and becomes creamy.
4. **Serve**: Divide the rice pudding into individual cups and let cool. Top with fresh fruit or berries, if desired.
5. **Enjoy**: Serve chilled or at room temperature.

www.ingramcontent.com/pod-product-compliance
Lightning Source LLC
LaVergne TN
LVHW081504060526
838201LV00056BA/2919